R AMAZING!™

We find the amazing in the ordinary everyday, with lists, polls and quizzes. Helping us to appreciate, in fun and quirky ways, the world in which we live.

Creating interactive content, R Amazing! is a safe place to explore different topics and share your views.

It is ok to disagree with us regarding who or what we think is amazing! We share our thoughts on our website and in our books to enable debate and discussion.

We encourage the expression of opinions in an appropriate way with an understanding that it is ok for people to have differing views.

R Amazing! debates should be conducted politely and respectfully, ending with an agreement and common ground, even if that is to agree to disagree.

www.r-amazing.com

Plants R Amazing!
Mark 'Markus' Baker & Adam Galvin

Published by R-and-Q.com.
Copyright © 2020 R-and-Q.com

PLANTS

R AMAZING!™

www.r-amazing.com/plants/

Adam Galvin and Markus Baker
Creators of R Amazing!

Please Note

Explanations of the words that are *highlighted* throughout
can be found at the back of this book in the glossary.

"*To plant a garden is to believe in tomorrow*"

Audrey Hepburn

"

Call a plant beautiful,
and it becomes a flower...

...Call it ugly, and it becomes a weed.

Jonathan Lockwood Huie

"

Darwin & Backster

Having written, 'On the Origin of Species', Darwin spent his remaining years exploring the life of plants. He concluded that all living things were linked by a common background (*ancestry*). His main discoveries were that plants cross *pollinate* to create new species. With a passion for how plants move, Darwin found that plants can 'see' the sun and grow towards it, calling this *phototropism*. He wrote extensively about this in his 1880 publication called, 'The Power of Movement in Plants'.

As you would expect, Darwin's findings were based on thorough scientific research that backed his conclusions and have inspired scientists to further explore plants today.

Someone else who has inspired a generation to look at plants differently was CIA interrogation specialist, Cleve Backster. A 1973 book and 1979 documentary titled, 'The Secret Life of Plants' shared many of Backster's experiments that suggested plants could sense intention and detect lies.

The academic and research community respect Darwin's exploration into plants but feel that Backster's experiments do not pass scientific scrutiny. His work is now seen more as *philosophical*, whereas Darwin's is still the foundation on which today's scientific plant research continues to be built upon. Both Darwin and Backster changed how many people look at plants and continue to inspire the next generation of scientists to either build upon or disprove their ideas and work.

Plant Neurobiology

A group of plant biologists looked to discover if plants exhibited any signs of *awareness*. They called this new field Plant Neurobiology and began to study how plants sense their surroundings to adapt and survive. This new area of plant science was met with both praise and criticism.

Some plant researchers and neuroscientists feel that the title 'Plant Neurobiology' does not make sense because plants do not have neurons. However, one of the main arguments for using the word '*neuro*' is that both plant and animal cells communicate with each other through the use of electrical signals.

Leading Plant Neurobiologist, Stefano Mancuso has shared how plants show behaviours similar to sleeping and playing. He also believes, that to protect our planet, plants should have rights, just like animals and humans do. These and other ideas are explored further in his books – The Revolutionary Genius of Plants and Brilliant Green: The Surprising History and Science of Plant Intelligence.

Intelligence is the ability to solve problems and plants are amazingly good in solving their problems.
Stefano Mancuso

DID YOU KNOW?

When touched the Mimosa pudica's leaves will fold inwards. This plant is sometimes called the touch-me-not plant, the sensitive plant or the tickle me plant.

Source: https://www.bbc.co.uk/news/uk-england-lincolnshire-17514950

Hence, a traveller should be a botanist, for in all views plants form the chief embellishment.

Charles Darwin

"

Awareness

Plant neurobiologist Stefano Mancuso suggests that many people believe plants are in a vegetative state when compared to humans and other animal species. On the surface, it appears that plants are not able to communicate and display no *awareness* of their surroundings. However, there is alot of evidence that suggests otherwise.

Researchers discovered that a single root tip can share up to 20 different chemicals with other plants. They can use these chemicals to warn other plants of potential threats! This suggests that plants are in fact aware of other plants and potential dangers.

Sunflowers interact and show *awareness* of the sun by following it through the sky from East to West. Likewise, the Poppy turns towards the sun and opens its petals, then closes them when the sun sets. Both of these examples show a level of interaction and *awareness* called positive *phototropism* (the position of a plant in response to light).

In his book, 'What a plant knows', Israeli botanist Daniel Chamovitz insists that plants, "see, feel, smell — and remember".

> *Plants are perfectly aware of themselves...My personal opinion is that there is no life that is not aware of itself.*
> Unknown

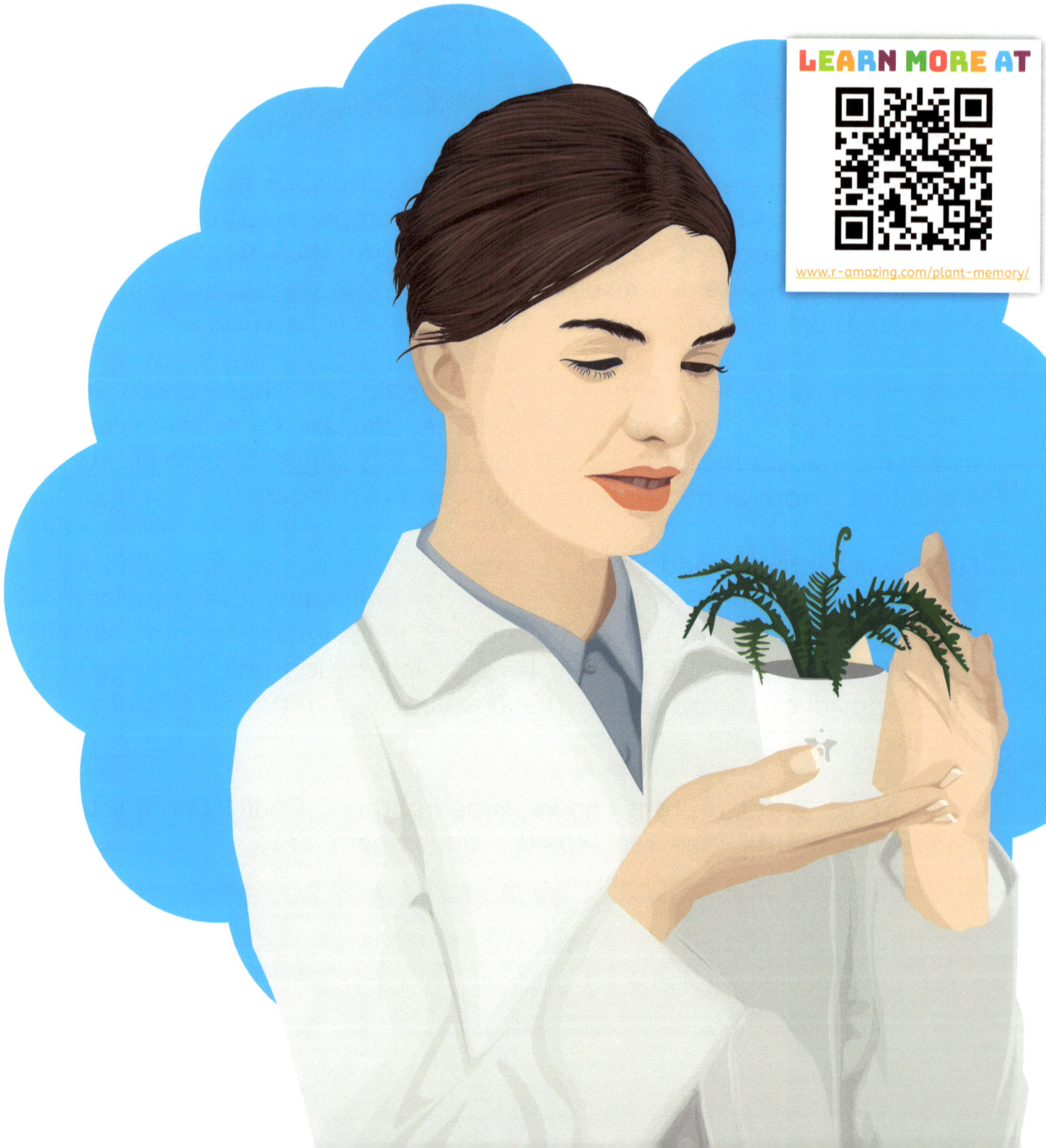

Memory

A 2014 study at the University of Western Australia, discovered the Mimosa pudcia can remember information for weeks, even if you change their living conditions. When touching or causing stress to the leaf for the first time it reacts and begins to close. However, when this exercise is repeated, the plant no longer reacts because it has learned that the touch or stress is not a threat. Thus demonstrating a form of short term memory.

Professor Martin Howard from the John Innes Centre, discovered how the Arabidopsis thaliana plant remembers cold winters to ensure that flowering doesn't begin until winter has passed. Even more impressive is that the plant can compute that if the winter is longer it will need to grow faster in the spring.

The Venus flytrap's *sensor* recognises 2 movements within 20 seconds before it traps its prey. This demonstrates that the plant holds a memory of 1 until its *sensor* is activated a second time.

This shows a plant can retain a memory of an event for a certain amount of time, before recalling that memory to deliver a specific response.

Plants are aware of their past
Daniel Chamovitz

"

*Like people, plants respond
to extra attention.*

H. Peter Loewer

DID YOU KNOW?

Phototropism is the term that describes the growth of a plant toward any light source. Heliotropism is the process that describes how a plant specifically tracks the sun's movement across the sky.

Communicating

Plants use a variety of ways to communicate, either through touch, their roots, excreting chemicals or even by working with *fungus*.

Most plants communicate using the *mycorrhizal network*. *Fungi*, in cooperation with plants, create an interconnected web that supports each other. This is sometimes called the 'Earth's natural internet'.

In 2010, Scientist Ren Sen Zeng experimented on pairs of tomato plants. He discovered that the pairs, which developed a *mycorrhizal network* between their roots, could defend themselves more effectively. They did this by exchanging nutrients and water, thus protecting themselves from drought.

Zeng explored this further by *infecting* one tomato plant of each pair with a *fungus* that caused *blight*. The uninfected plant of the pairs were less likely to catch the infection if they were part of the *mycorrhizal network*. Those uninfected plants were able to do this by receiving the infected plant's defense responses through 'Earth's natural internet'.

Plants communicate to defend themselves, ask for assistance and understand their surroundings.

Venus Flytrap

All plants need water, *gases* and sunlight to survive, however *carnivorous* plants like the venus flytrap also require meat to stay alive.

Charles Darwin wrote that the Venus flytrap is "one of the most wonderful [plants] in the world." They have a lifespan of 20 years or longer and bloom year after year.

Venus flytraps are not huge plants, they grow to around 13 centimeters (5 inches) in *diameter*. They are quite amazing, which is probably why Darwin found them so fascinating.

Flytraps entice insects by secreting a sweet smelling *nectar*. When bugs land inside the open jaws of the flytrap, sensory hairs inside of the petals track and count the movements of the insect. Cleverly, if it detects 2 or more motions (in 20 seconds) it traps the insect by rapidly clamping its jaws together. It is sealed airtight so no *bacteria* can get into the plant. By having this mechanism of counting movements within 20 seconds it stops the Venus flytrap capturing dirt or other items that are not healthy for it to swallow.

Digestive juices are secreted to start breaking down the insect until only the parts of the bug that can't be consumed are left. This takes around 12 days, after which the Venus flytrap will open its jaws and discard the remaining body parts.

DID YOU KNOW?

When viewed from below most climbing beans grow up around their pole anticlockwise. That is all except the runner beans which are unique by growing up their poles towards the sun in a clockwise manner.

Source: https://www.theatlantic.com/science/archive/2019/03/whitefly-infestation-plant-chemicals/585637/

Plants look after us if we look after them.
Unknown

34

21

5

3

1 2

8

13

Golden Ratio In Plants

Beauty is said to have a mathematical formula. For at least the last 4,000 years objects have been designed by humans to look *aesthetically* pleasing by using the Golden Ratio.

The fibonacci sequence is the building block of how we understand the Golden Ratio and works by adding the two previous numbers together to get the next digit, like this: 0+1= 1, 1+1=2, 1+2=3, 2+3=5, 3+5=8 5+8=13 8+13=21 13+21=34 etc. When constructed together as squares, these numbers create a rectangle that has the Golden Ratio of 1.618. For example, if the width is 1, the height will be 1.618. Then, by drawing a line through each square that builds the rectangle, a golden ratio spiral is created (see picture). This spiral naturally draws your eye in towards the focal point.

Nature has always used the Golden Ratio, its rectangles and spirals to create beautiful things, especially in the plant world. For example, the number of petals on a plant is generally a fibonacci number. Lilies and Iris have 3 petals, Buttercups and Pinks have 5 petals and Daisies can often be found with 21, 34 or 55 petals.

The spiraled centre of a sunflower is also formed around the fibonacci sequence and the golden ratio. As too are the curls of the *fronds* of a young fern, the stalks of the comfrey flower, the way the aloe plant grows and the bases of pine cones.

Defending & Protecting

Because plants are rooted to the earth and cannot run away they have to try to defend and protect themselves in other ways.

Here are the top 5 ways plants do this:

1. They have *armature* - Some species of plants have thorns, spines, prickles and *trichomes*. Their role in providing protection is quite self-evident: they are sharp, stabby and can impale predators.

2. They choke their predators - when insects try to eat them, the plants release *hydrogen cyanide*, which makes the insects choke until they eventually stop breathing.

3. They induce a heart attack - the foxglove plant contains a potent *toxin* known as digitoxin. Eating any part of this plant can potentially lead to heart failure.

4. They pretend to be rocks - pebble plants adapt to look like rocks. They are able to *camouflage* themselves by blending into their environment to avoid being eaten.

5. They form partnerships with ants - The ants protect them against potential threats, and in return the ants get a place to live and food to eat.

"

Eat food. Not too much.
Mostly plants.

Michael Pollan

DID YOU KNOW?

Ahhh! Screamed the plant! When bitten by insects, plants can release a scream of airborne chemicals. They do this to tell other plants to up their defenses to protect themselves from being bitten too. As humans we can't pick up the plant's signals, but to plants, their messages are received loud and clear.

Can plants hear?

Charles Darwin once noted that seedlings appeared to be sensitive to the vibrations of sound. Intrigued, Darwin was motivated to explore this further. He even encouraged his son, Francis to play his bassoon to the plants. Even though Darwin's results were inconclusive, they did inspire others to continue his research into plant's ability to hear.

Plant neurobiologist Stefano Mancuso explains that plants are extremely good at detecting certain sounds and *frequencies*. If a 200hz or 300hz sound is placed near the roots of a plant, they will follow it, believing it to be the sound of water.

In 2014, scientists discovered that the sound of a caterpillar chewing its leaf caused the thale cress to release a defensive chemical, thus protecting it from another attack.

Maybe the idea of plants responding to the sound of a song or musical instrument may not be such a crazy idea after all!

> *We have identified that plants respond to sound and they make their own sounds.*
> Monica Gagliano

Healing Plants

Although a plant to heal every illness may well exist, not all of them have yet been found. However, there are many plants that do help with human recovery. Although we know the positive effects that eating plants like fruit and vegetables can have on our bodies, we may not be so aware of the healing effects of some other plants.

Throughout history there are many examples of the healing power of plants. Even as far back as 1500 B.C. medicinal herbs were found in the personal effects of Ötzi the Iceman. In their medical texts, known as *Ebers Papyrus*, the Egyptians shared healing information on more than 850 plants, which includes some that are still used to this day like garlic, juniper, cannabis, castor bean, aloe, and mandrake.

Today there are many herbalists and *naturopathic* doctors who help their patients with medicine that has been grown in the ground. Some examples of how plants can help us are:

- Peppermint – digestion and sore muscles.
- Chamomile – sleep and reduces anxiety.
- Lavender – relaxation, comfort & reduces infection.

> *For every human illness, somewhere in the world there exists a plant which is the cure.*
> Rudolf Steiner

DID YOU KNOW?

THESE PLANTS CAN KILL

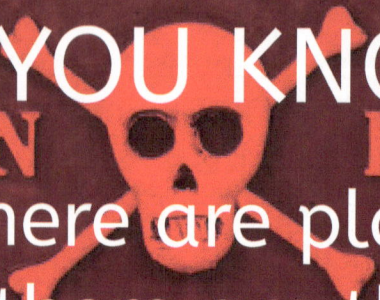

Just as there are plants that can heal there are those that can kill. The Poison Garden in England shares plants that can kill humans.
So enter with caution.

Plants are solar powered air purifiers whose filter never needs replacing.

Khang Kijarro Nguyen

"

Compliments

Insults

Feelings

Plants know when they're being touched and can tell the difference between hot and cold.

Researcher Diana Bowles discovered that when a tomato plant leaf was burnt it would warn the other leaves of the danger. She *hypothesised* that the message is sent from the wounded leaf to the unwounded leaves. When tested, they found the tomato plant responded to the hot metal by warning its other leaves of a potentially dangerous environment. It did this by sending out an electrical signal that could even be picked up at a distance.

Plants can even recognise the slightest of touches, when researchers discovered that the vines from the Bur cucumber can feel the touch of string that weighs just 0.25 gram (0.009 ounce). This is equivalent to weight of just 1 grain of rice.

In 2018, an interesting experiment carried out by the furniture store IKEA suggested that plants can, somehow, pick up and react to human emotions and feelings. By placing two identical potted plants in a school, researchers tasked students to send one of the plants nothing but compliments and the other nothing but insults for 30 days. The results were astounding! The plant which had been insulted became droopy, withered and dying. In comparison, the plant that received the positive emotions and feelings was much healthier.

"

My fake plants died because I did not pretend to water them.

Mitch Hedberg

DID YOU KNOW?

Taking around seven to ten years to bloom, the Carrion flowers are sometimes known as the world's worst smelling flower because it smells like rotting flesh. Hence this plant being known as the corpse or stinking flower!

Source: https://listverse.com/2013/04/08/10-weird-and-truly-terrifying-plants/ & https://en.wikipedia.org/wiki/Carrion_flower

My picture of the most amazing plant in the world!

The most amazing plant in the world is

. . . .

My favourite part of this amazing plant is...

....

....

....

....

....

....

This plant is amazing because...

....

....

....

....

Glossary

Aesthetically - in a way that gives pleasure through beauty.

Armature - protective covering, like amour.

Ancestry - the origin or background of something.

Awareness - the ability to see, hear, feel or experience the world.

Bacteria - tiny organisms that are everywhere and can cause diseases.

Blight - disease, typically caused by some fungi.

Camouflage - to blend in to the surroundings.

Carnivorous - something that eats meat.

Diameter - straight line passing through the centre of a circle or sphere.

Ebers Papyrus - 1550 BC Egyptian medical paper about herbalism.

Frequencies -the rate per second of a vibration constituting in a wave.

Fronds - the leaf parts of a palm, fern, or similar plant.

Fungus/Fungi - living organisms such as yeasts and moulds.

Gases - substance, like air that is neither solid nor liquid.

Heliotropism – how a plant tracks the sun's movement across the sky.

Hydrogen cyanide – highly volatile, colourless & poisonous liquid.

Hypothesised – to give a possible but yet unproven idea.

Infecting – to pass a disease to another.

Mycorrhizal Network – relationship between fungus and plants.

Naturopathic – system of treating diseases using natural methods.

Nectar – sweet liquid produced by flowers and plants.

Neuro – relating to nerves or the nervous system.

Philosophical – the exploration of knowledge, reality, and existence.

Phototropism – the growth of a plant toward any light source.

Pollinate – deposits pollen to allow fertilisation.

Sensor – a device which can respond to heat, light, sound, pressure or motion.

Toxin – a poison.

Trichomes – small hair or fine outgrowth on a plant.

MORE BOOKS BY R&Q

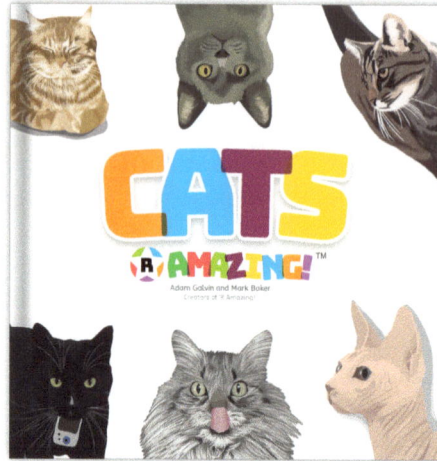

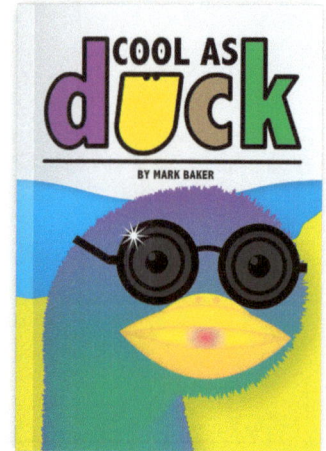

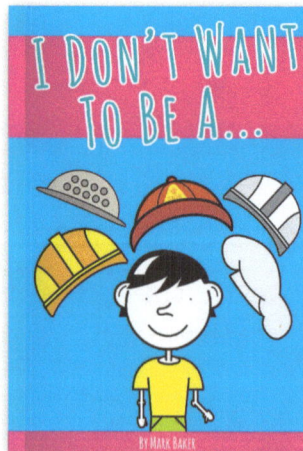

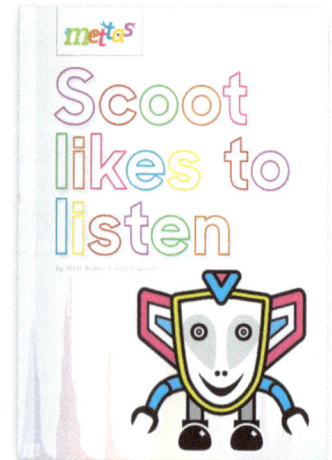

DOOR KNOB FOR A NOSE
BY MARK BAKER & JENNIFER BAKER

CATS R AMAZING!™
Adam Galvin and Mark Baker

COOL AS duck
BY MARK BAKER

I DON'T WANT TO BE A...
BY MARK BAKER

THIS BOOK NEVER ENDS...™
...it keeps looping round and round until somebody says "PLEASE STOP READING NOW!"

Who is going to give up first? The grown up or the child because...

By Mark Baker

mettos
Scoot likes to listen
By Mark Baker & ...

www.ingramcontent.com/pod-product-compliance
Lightning Source LLC
Chambersburg PA
CBHW060832270326
41933CB00002B/54